The Invention of Surgery

By Gyanvriksha Publications

Gyanvriksha Publication

ज्ञानोद्याने, पुस्तक सर्वे बीजम्

Gyanvriksha Publication

ज्ञानोद्याने, पुस्तकं सर्वं बीजम्

For permission requests, please write to the publisher at the Email below:

Gyanvriksha Publications

Email: gyanvrikshapublications@gmail.com

First Edition - 2024

Disclaimer

The content presented in "The Invention of Surgery" is intended for informational and educational purposes only. While we strive to provide accurate and up-to-date information, the field of surgery is continuously evolving, and new discoveries and advancements may not be reflected in this book.

The authors and Gyanvriksha Publications make no representations or warranties regarding the completeness, reliability, or accuracy of the information contained herein. This book is not a substitute for professional medical advice, diagnosis, or treatment. Always seek the advice of qualified healthcare professionals with any questions you may have regarding a medical condition or treatment.

The views and opinions expressed in this book are those of the authors and do not necessarily reflect the views of Gyanvriksha Publications. The publication of this book does not imply endorsement of any specific medical practices or technologies.

For any inquiries or further information, please contact us at:

Email: gyanvrikshapublications@gmail.com

Thank you for your understanding and for choosing to engage with the fascinating world of surgical innovation through our publication.

Acknowledgement

With great warmth and gratitude, we reach the end of this journey and want to acknowledge the many incredible people who have helped make "The Invention of Surgery" a reality. This book is a testament to the collective effort and passion of everyone involved, and we couldn't have done it without you.

First, a heartfelt thank you goes to the medical professionals and historians who have generously shared their wisdom and insights. Your expertise and dedication have been the backbone of this book, and your willingness to share your knowledge has deeply inspired us. We are especially grateful to the surgeons, researchers, and educators who took the time to offer their perspectives, enriching our understanding of this remarkable field.

To our editorial team, we extend our deepest appreciation. Your keen eye, thoughtful feedback, and commitment to excellence have been invaluable. You've helped transform our ideas into a polished work, ensuring that every detail was meticulously addressed. Your hard work and dedication have been truly extraordinary.

We also want to give a big shoutout to our graphic designers and layout experts. Your creativity and talent have brought this book to life visually, making complex concepts easier to grasp and engaging for our readers. Your designs have added a special touch that we are truly grateful for.

To our families and friends, your unwavering support has been our anchor throughout this endeavour. Your encouragement, patience, and belief in our vision have been a source of strength. Thank you for standing by us and for your understanding during the long hours of work.

And finally, to our readers, we are profoundly thankful for your interest in "The Invention of Surgery." We hope that this book not only deepens your appreciation for the evolution of surgical practices but also inspires you to marvel at the remarkable advancements that continue to shape this field.

With heartfelt thanks,

Team Gyanvriksha Publications
Email: gyanvrikshapublications@gmail.com

Contents

Prologue

The Dawn of Surgical Innovation

Excerpt:

Surgery, a field that once relied on the skill of the hands and the sharpness of the mind, has evolved into a domain where technology and human ingenuity converge to create miracles. As we embark on this exploration of the "Invention of Surgery," we will uncover the fascinating journey from primitive practices to the sophisticated techniques of today. This prologue sets the stage for a deeper understanding of how surgery has transformed over the centuries and why it holds such a profound place in the annals of medical history.

In this prologue, we will explore:

1. **The Origins of Surgical Practice:** How early humans began to practice surgery with rudimentary tools and techniques.
2. **The Evolution of Surgical Knowledge:** How the understanding of anatomy and surgical techniques developed over time.
3. **Key Milestones in Surgical Innovation:** The significant breakthroughs that shaped the modern practice of surgery.

4. **The Intersection of Science and Art:** How surgery blends scientific advancements with the artistry of precise craftsmanship.
5. **The Promise of Future Discoveries:** What lies ahead in the ever-evolving field of surgery and how it continues to push boundaries.

The Complete Prologue:

The Origins of Surgical Practice: How Early Humans Began to Practice Surgery with Rudimentary Tools and Techniques

Surgery's roots stretch back to ancient times, where the practice was often intertwined with mysticism and rudimentary medical knowledge. Early humans, driven by necessity and curiosity, began to experiment with basic surgical techniques to treat injuries and illnesses. Stone tools and sharpened bones were among the earliest instruments used for these procedures, and evidence of their use has been found in archeological sites dating back thousands of years.

The practice of surgery in ancient civilizations, such as Egypt, India, and Greece, provides a glimpse into the early attempts at healing. Ancient Egyptian texts describe surgical procedures performed with a mix of practical techniques and spiritual beliefs. Indian surgeons like Sushruta wrote detailed texts on surgical practices, including techniques for cataract surgery and the use of sutures. In Greece, Hippocrates and his followers laid the groundwork for surgical knowledge, emphasizing the importance of careful observation and systematic treatment.

Despite the limited tools and knowledge of the time, these early practices laid the foundation for the development of surgery as a scientific discipline. The challenges faced by ancient surgeons and their ingenuity in overcoming them are a testament to the enduring human drive to heal and improve lives.

The Evolution of Surgical Knowledge: How the Understanding of Anatomy and Surgical Techniques Developed Over Time

As societies advanced, so did the understanding of human anatomy and the methods used in surgery. The Middle Ages saw limited progress due to religious and societal constraints, but the Renaissance marked a period of significant advancement. Pioneering figures such as Andreas Vesalius revolutionized the study of anatomy through detailed dissections and accurate anatomical drawings, which provided a clearer understanding of the human body.

During this time, surgical techniques began to evolve from the use of basic tools to more refined instruments. The invention of the **scalpel**, **forceps**, and **surgical scissors** marked a new era in surgery, allowing for greater precision and effectiveness in procedures.

The 19th century brought further advancements with the development of **aseptic techniques** and

anesthesia. Joseph Lister's work on antiseptic practices dramatically reduced surgical infections, while the introduction of anesthesia allowed patients to undergo surgery without the agony of pain.

The evolution of surgical knowledge continued into the 20th and 21st centuries, with the development of **minimally invasive techniques**, **robotic surgery**, and **advanced imaging technologies**. Each of these advancements has contributed to a deeper understanding of the human body and has transformed surgical practice.

Key Milestones in Surgical Innovation: The Significant Breakthroughs That Shaped the Modern Practice of Surgery

Several key milestones have marked the progress of surgical innovation, each representing a leap forward in the field. The development of **anesthesia** in the 19th century was a groundbreaking advancement, allowing surgeons to perform complex procedures with the patient in a state of unconsciousness, free from pain.

The discovery of **antiseptics** by Joseph Lister revolutionized infection control in surgery, dramatically reducing post-operative complications and saving countless lives. Lister's techniques laid the groundwork for modern sterile practices, which are fundamental to today's surgical procedures.

The 20th century saw the advent of **minimally invasive surgery** techniques, such as laparoscopic surgery. These procedures, performed through small incisions using specialized instruments, offer patients shorter recovery times, reduced pain, and minimal scarring.

In recent decades, **robotic surgery** and **computer-assisted techniques** have further transformed the field. Robotic systems, such as the da Vinci Surgical System, enable surgeons to perform delicate procedures with extraordinary precision and control. **3D imaging**, **augmented reality**, and **artificial intelligence** are also pushing the boundaries of what is possible, enhancing surgical accuracy and patient outcomes.

The Intersection of Science and Art: How Surgery Blends Scientific Advancements with the Artistry of Precise Craftsmanship

Surgery is a unique blend of science and art, where precise techniques and advanced technologies intersect with the surgeon's skill and artistry. The scientific advancements in surgical tools and techniques provide the foundation for modern procedures, but the execution of these techniques requires a high degree of craftsmanship and expertise.

The artistry of surgery lies in the surgeon's ability to navigate complex anatomical structures, make critical decisions, and perform intricate maneuvers with precision. This combination of scientific knowledge and artistic skill defines the practice of surgery and highlights the importance of both technical expertise and human touch in achieving successful outcomes.

The Promise of Future Discoveries: What Lies Ahead in the Ever-Evolving Field of Surgery and How It Continues to Push Boundaries

The future of surgery holds exciting possibilities as new discoveries and technologies continue to emerge. Advances in **genetic engineering**, **regenerative medicine**, and **nanotechnology** offer the potential to revolutionize surgical practice and patient care.

Genetic engineering may enable personalized treatments and the development of therapies tailored to individual genetic profiles, while **regenerative medicine** holds promise for repairing or replacing damaged tissues and organs. **Nanotechnology** could lead to innovations in minimally invasive procedures and targeted drug delivery.

As we look ahead, the field of surgery will continue to evolve, driven by ongoing research and technological advancements. The integration of these new discoveries will shape the future of surgical practice, enhancing capabilities, improving outcomes, and expanding access to care.

Conclusion:

The prologue to the "Invention of Surgery" provides a glimpse into the rich history and dynamic evolution of this vital field. From its humble beginnings with primitive tools to the sophisticated techniques of today, surgery has been marked by a continuous journey of discovery and innovation.

The interplay between scientific advancements and the artistry of surgical practice reflects the enduring human quest to heal and improve lives. As we explore the history and future of surgery, we recognize the profound impact that these advancements have had and will continue to have on the world of medicine.

Prologue: A Slice Through Time

- **Explanation:** Imagine you're living thousands of years ago. People had to figure out how to survive when someone got hurt or sick. They didn't have the knowledge or tools we do today, but they were curious and brave enough to start exploring. This introduction takes you on a journey from those first curious attempts to understand the human body, leading to what we now call surgery. We'll begin by looking at how surgery started as a basic survival skill and grew into a highly advanced medical practice.

Chapter 1: Ancient Beginnings: The Dawn of Surgical Practice

- **Explanation:** Long before we had hospitals and modern medicine, people still needed to fix injuries or deal with illnesses. This chapter looks at how early humans performed surgery using the simplest tools they could find, like sharp stones or bones. It's about understanding how our ancestors, driven by necessity and curiosity, started performing the first surgeries—even if they were basic and often dangerous.

Chapter 2: The Tools of the Trade: From Flint to Scalpel

- **Explanation:** Surgery couldn't happen without tools. In this chapter, we'll explore how the instruments used in surgery have evolved over time. We'll start with the crude tools made from flint or bone and follow their transformation into the precise surgical instruments we use today, like scalpels and forceps. This chapter is like a history lesson on how technology has improved the way surgeons can work.

Chapter 3: The First Surgeons: Heroes or Butchers?

- **Explanation:** Being a surgeon wasn't always a respected job. In ancient times, people often feared surgeons because their methods were painful and dangerous. This chapter explores who these early surgeons were and how they were seen by society. Were they brave heroes saving lives, or were they seen as butchers who caused more harm than good? We'll look at the ethical challenges they faced and how their role evolved over time.

Chapter 4: The Renaissance Revolution: Rebirth of Surgical Art

- **Explanation:** During the Renaissance, a period of great learning and discovery, surgery started to change dramatically. This chapter explains how surgery transformed from a rough and often brutal practice into a respected science. We'll learn about the people who made this possible—pioneers who challenged old beliefs and brought new knowledge to the world, helping to make surgery more effective and less terrifying.

Chapter 5: Pain and Progress: The Birth of Anesthesia

- **Explanation:** Can you imagine having surgery without any pain relief? Before anesthesia, that was the reality. Surgery was excruciatingly painful, and many people didn't survive because of the shock. This chapter tells the story of how the discovery of anesthesia—a way to numb the body during surgery—changed everything. It made surgery more humane and allowed surgeons to perform more complex procedures, paving the way for modern medicine.

Chapter 6: Blood and Guts: Understanding Infection and Sterilization

- **Explanation:** In the past, even if a surgery went well, many patients would die afterward because of infections. People didn't yet understand how germs caused disease, so they didn't know how to keep wounds clean. This chapter covers the battle to control infection and how sterilization techniques were developed. These advancements turned surgery from a risky last resort into a safer, life-saving practice.

Chapter 7: The Miracle of Transplantation: Borrowed Life

- **Explanation:** Transplant surgery is one of the most incredible achievements in medicine. This chapter explores how doctors learned to take organs from one person and place them into another. It's about the first successful transplants, the challenges of preventing the body from rejecting a new organ, and the ethical questions that come with such procedures. This is where science meets moral dilemmas in the quest to save lives.

Chapter 8: Robotics and Beyond: The Future of Surgery

- **Explanation:** Technology is constantly changing the way we do things, and surgery is no exception. This chapter looks at the role of robotics and artificial intelligence in the future of surgery. We'll explore how these advanced tools are helping surgeons perform operations with incredible precision and what this means for the future of healthcare.

Chapter 9: Surgeons of the Future: A New Breed of Healers

- **Explanation:** As surgery continues to evolve, so does the role of the surgeon. This chapter discusses how modern surgeons are not just skilled with their hands but also need to be compassionate, understanding the emotional needs of their patients. We'll look at how surgeons are trained today and what skills they need to meet the challenges of tomorrow's healthcare.

Epilogue: The Human Touch: Why Surgery Will Always Be an Art

- **Explanation:** Even with all the technological advancements, surgery will always be a deeply human practice. This closing chapter reflects on why the human touch—compassion, intuition, and the art of healing—remains crucial in surgery. Despite all the machines and technology, the relationship between a surgeon and their patient is at the heart of every operation. This chapter leaves us with an appreciation for the art of surgery, reminding us that it's not just about cutting and stitching, but about caring and healing.

Chapter 1

Ancient Beginnings: The Dawn of Surgical Practice

Excerpt:

In the beginning, surgery wasn't the sophisticated science we know today. It was raw, risky, and often a matter of life or death. Imagine living in a time when the only tools available were sharp stones, and the only anaesthesia was the strength of your own will. Early humans, driven by necessity and curiosity, performed surgeries that, while primitive, laid the groundwork for the medical advances we benefit from today.

In this chapter, we will explore:

1. **The First Surgeons:** Who were they?
2. **Tools and Techniques:** What did they use?
3. **Survival and Superstition:** How did beliefs influence early practices?
4. **Milestones in Ancient Surgery:** Key events that changed everything.

The Complete Chapter:

The First Surgeons: Who Were They?

Imagine a world where survival was a daily challenge. Injuries from hunting, accidents, or conflict were common, and the risk of infection or death was high. Early humans didn't have the luxury of modern medicine, but they did have something incredibly powerful: the instinct to survive and the curiosity to find solutions.

The first "surgeons" weren't trained doctors but were likely the elders or healers in their communities. These individuals had knowledge passed down through generations, often based on trial and error. They were the ones who took on the responsibility of treating wounds, setting broken bones, and even performing rudimentary surgeries, like trepanation—a procedure where a hole was drilled into the skull, possibly to relieve pressure or release evil spirits. This wasn't done lightly, and those who survived were often seen as chosen or special.

Tools and Techniques: What Did They Use?

When we think of surgery today, we imagine sterile operating rooms and precise instruments. But thousands of years ago, things were very different. The earliest tools were made from materials like flint, obsidian, and bone. These tools were sharp enough to cut skin and flesh, though the procedures were far from painless or safe.

One of the most common tools was a sharp stone, used for making incisions or scraping away damaged tissue. Another was a piece of bone, shaped into a primitive needle for stitching wounds together with sinew or plant fibers. The techniques were crude, but they were the first steps toward understanding how to treat injuries and illnesses.

Imagine a healer in a small, prehistoric community, using a sharpened piece of flint to remove an infected tooth or cut away dead flesh from a wound. Without antiseptics or pain relief, these early surgeries were excruciatingly painful, and survival was never guaranteed. Yet, these early surgeons persevered because they understood that sometimes, cutting into the body was the only way to save a life.

Survival and Superstition: How Did Beliefs Influence Early Practices?

In these ancient times, surgery wasn't just about science—because, in truth, science as we know it didn't exist yet. It was deeply intertwined with religion and superstition. People believed that illnesses and injuries were often the result of evil spirits, curses, or the wrath of the gods.

Therefore, the act of performing surgery wasn't just a physical task but a spiritual one.

Before a surgery, rituals and prayers were often performed to appease the gods or ward off evil spirits. The healers themselves were sometimes considered shamans or spiritual leaders, believed to have special powers to communicate with the divine. In some cases, the surgical tools were seen as sacred objects, blessed by rituals before they were used.

This combination of survival instincts and spiritual beliefs meant that early surgery was as much about faith as it was about practicality. Despite the pain and risks, people were willing to undergo these procedures because they believed it was their best chance at survival—and possibly redemption.

Milestones in Ancient Surgery: Key Events That Changed Everything

Throughout history, there were key moments when surgery took significant leaps forward, even in these ancient times. One of the earliest recorded surgeries was trepanation, the act of drilling or scraping a hole into the skull. Remarkably, evidence shows that some people survived this procedure, as seen in the regrowth of bone around the opening.

Another milestone was the development of techniques to set broken bones. Early surgeons learned to use splints made from wood or bark to keep fractures in place while they healed. This practice significantly improved the chances of recovery from injuries that would otherwise have been fatal or disabling.

Over time, these rudimentary practices spread across different cultures, each adding their own innovations. In ancient Egypt, for example, the Edwin Smith Papyrus—a medical text dating back to around 1600 BCE—documents surgical techniques for treating wounds and fractures. This papyrus is one of the oldest known medical documents and shows that even then, there was a systematic approach to surgery.

Conclusion:

The dawn of surgical practice was a time of incredible courage and ingenuity. Without the knowledge we have today, early humans were willing to risk everything to find ways to heal and survive. Their efforts laid the foundation for the advanced surgical techniques we now take for granted.

As you read through this chapter, try to imagine the challenges these early surgeons faced. Think about the courage it took to cut into a living body with nothing but a sharp stone and a prayer. It's a testament to the enduring human spirit—the same spirit that drives us to continue exploring, discovering, and pushing the boundaries of what's possible in the field of surgery.

Chapter 2

The Tools of the Trade: From Flint to Scalpel

Excerpt:

The story of surgery is not just about the brave individuals who performed it but also about the tools they used. From the sharp edges of flint and obsidian to the precision of modern scalpels, the evolution of surgical instruments tells a fascinating tale of innovation, trial, and error. Each tool, no matter how simple or sophisticated, played a crucial role in the survival and progress of humanity.

In this chapter, we will explore:

1. **The Birth of Surgical Tools:** How did it all begin?
2. **From Stones to Metal:** The evolution of materials.
3. **The Role of Innovation:** Key inventions that changed surgery forever.
4. **The Scalpel's Journey:** How a simple blade became a symbol of modern surgery.

The Complete Chapter:

The Birth of Surgical Tools: How Did It All Begin?

Imagine yourself thousands of years ago, in a world where survival was a constant battle. You're faced with an injured person—perhaps a family member or a fellow hunter—who has a deep wound that could easily become infected. What would you do? The need to act quickly and effectively led early humans to develop the first surgical tools.

The earliest tools were born out of necessity. Sharp stones, particularly flint and obsidian, were some of the first materials used for cutting. These stones could be chipped into sharp edges that were effective for making incisions or scraping away damaged tissue. Although primitive, these tools were the beginning of surgical instruments—crude yet life-saving in their own way.

These early tools weren't just about functionality; they were also deeply symbolic. In many ancient cultures, tools used for surgery were considered sacred. Healers often performed rituals before using them, believing that these tools were instruments of the gods, meant to bridge the gap between the physical and spiritual worlds.

From Stones to Metal: The Evolution of Materials

As human civilization advanced, so did the materials used for surgical tools. The discovery of metals like bronze and iron marked a significant turning point. Metal tools were sharper, more durable, and could be crafted with greater precision than their stone predecessors.

Bronze was one of the first metals to be used in surgical instruments. Ancient civilizations, such as the Egyptians and the Greeks, began to forge bronze scalpels, needles, and forceps. These tools were more refined and allowed for more complex surgical procedures. Imagine the difference between using a jagged stone and a finely crafted bronze scalpel—this evolution made surgeries more effective and less traumatic.

Iron, and later steel, further revolutionized surgical instruments. Steel's ability to hold a sharp edge made it the material of choice for scalpels, which became the surgeon's most trusted tool. The precision and reliability of steel instruments allowed surgeons to perform more delicate and intricate operations, opening up new possibilities for medical treatment.

The Role of Innovation: Key Inventions That Changed Surgery Forever

Throughout history, certain key inventions have propelled the field of surgery forward. One such innovation was the invention of the surgical needle. Before the advent of metal needles, early surgeons used bone or thorn needles to sew wounds. The introduction of metal needles, along with sutures made from materials like catgut, transformed wound closure and reduced the risk of infection.

Another groundbreaking invention was the surgical saw, developed in the Middle Ages. Used primarily for amputations, the surgical saw allowed surgeons to remove damaged limbs more efficiently, often saving the patient's life by preventing the spread of infection. Though the procedure was brutal by today's standards, it was a significant advancement in surgical practice.

The development of forceps, scissors, and clamps further advanced surgical techniques. These tools gave surgeons greater control and precision, allowing them to perform complex procedures with less damage to surrounding tissues. With each new invention, surgery became more sophisticated, less painful, and more successful.

The Scalpel's Journey: How a Simple Blade Became a Symbol of Modern Surgery

The scalpel is perhaps the most iconic surgical instrument, symbolizing precision, skill, and the art of healing. But the journey of the scalpel is one of humble beginnings.

In ancient times, the scalpel was a simple blade made from stone, then bronze, and later steel. Over the centuries, its design has been refined to meet the needs of increasingly complex surgical procedures. Today's scalpel is a finely balanced, incredibly sharp instrument that allows surgeons to make precise cuts with minimal damage to tissues.

But the scalpel is more than just a tool—it's a symbol of the surgeon's craft. It represents the balance between life and death, the delicate dance of saving lives through skilful intervention. In the hands of a skilled surgeon, the scalpel is an extension of the mind and body, a tool that can heal and transform.

Conclusion:

The tools of surgery have come a long way from the sharp stones of our ancestors. Each innovation, each new material, and each refinement of design has brought us closer to the sophisticated surgical practices we have today. But beyond the technical advancements, these tools tell a story of human ingenuity, persistence, and the unrelenting drive to overcome the challenges of survival.

As you think about the evolution of surgical tools, consider the courage it took to use them in the early days of medicine. Imagine the healer, holding a sharp piece of flint, about to perform a life-saving procedure with nothing but their wits and the primitive tools at their disposal. Their bravery and creativity laid the foundation for the advanced surgical techniques that save lives today.

In many ways, the story of surgical tools is the story of humanity itself—a story of growth, learning, and the endless quest to improve and innovate.

Chapter 3

The First Surgeons: Heroes or Butchers?

Excerpt:

In ancient times, surgery was a double-edged sword—both literally and figuratively. The brave individuals who attempted these early procedures were often seen as either miracle workers or feared as butchers. Without the benefits of modern anaesthesia or antibiotics, surgery was as much about courage as it was about skill. But who were these early surgeons, and how did they navigate the fine line between saving a life and taking one?

In this chapter, we will explore:

1. **The Role of the Healer:** Who were the first surgeons?
2. **Life or Death:** The risks and rewards of ancient surgery.
3. **Public Perception:** Were they revered or reviled?
4. **Ethical Dilemmas:** The moral challenges they faced.

The Complete Chapter:

The Role of the Healer: Who Were the First Surgeons?

Imagine living in a time when there was no formal medical training, no hospitals, and no standard practices for treating injuries or diseases. In this world, the role of the surgeon often fell to the local healer, shaman, or barber. These individuals were not trained in the way modern doctors are, but they possessed knowledge passed down through generations, often blending practical experience with spiritual beliefs.

The first surgeons were more than just practitioners of medicine—they were the community's problem solvers. When someone was injured in a battle or a hunting accident, the healer was called upon to treat the wound. When a severe infection threatened a person's life, the healer might be asked to perform a dangerous procedure to try and save them. These early surgeons had to be resourceful, using whatever tools and materials they had on hand to perform their work.

These healers often had to make quick decisions in life-or-death situations, relying on their intuition and experience. Their work was as much an art as it was a science, blending the physical with the spiritual in a way that modern medicine often overlooks. In many cultures, these healers were respected and even feared, as their knowledge gave them power over life and death.

Life or Death: The Risks and Rewards of Ancient Surgery

Surgery in ancient times was an incredibly risky endeavor. Without anesthesia, patients had to endure unimaginable pain during procedures. The absence of antiseptics meant that even a successful surgery could be followed by a fatal infection. Every surgery was a gamble, with the odds often stacked against the patient.

Despite these risks, the rewards could be immense. For those who survived, surgery could mean the difference between life and death, or the ability to continue living without debilitating pain or disability. Imagine a soldier with a shattered limb after a battle; a successful amputation could save his life, even if it meant living with a severe handicap. For the patient, the surgeon's skill was often their last hope.

However, the line between a life-saving hero and a butcher was thin. A single mistake could turn a routine procedure into a fatal disaster. Surgeons often worked under immense pressure, knowing that their reputation—and the lives of their patients—hung in the balance with every cut they made. Despite their best efforts, the high mortality rate associated with surgery meant that these early practitioners often found themselves feared as much as they were respected.

Public Perception: Were They Revered or Reviled?

Public perception of early surgeons varied widely depending on the outcomes of their work and the culture they lived in. In some societies, successful surgeons were revered as miracle workers, their names remembered for generations. In others, surgeons who failed—or who were perceived as causing more harm than good—were reviled, sometimes even punished or ostracized.

In ancient Rome, for example, surgeons who performed well were rewarded with fame and wealth. Their skills were sought after by the elite, and successful procedures could lead to significant social standing. However, a botched surgery could ruin a surgeon's reputation, leading to exile or worse. The same was true in other ancient cultures, where the line between success and failure was razor-thin.

The tension between reverence and revulsion also extended to the broader community. Surgery was often seen as a last resort, and those who underwent it were sometimes viewed with a mix of pity and fear. A successful surgery might be celebrated, but a failure could lead to the surgeon being labeled as a butcher—a person who caused unnecessary suffering. This duality made the life of an early surgeon both exhilarating and perilous.

Ethical Dilemmas: The Moral Challenges They Faced

The first surgeons faced a range of ethical dilemmas that resonate even today. One of the most significant challenges was the question of consent. In a time before informed consent was a recognized concept, many patients underwent surgery because they had no other choice or because they were pressured by family or community leaders. This raised serious ethical questions about autonomy and the right to refuse treatment.

Another dilemma was the balance between doing harm and doing good. Surgeons often had to weigh the potential benefits of a procedure against the likely pain and suffering it would cause. Without modern pain management techniques, surgery was almost guaranteed to be a traumatic experience. Surgeons had to decide whether the potential outcome justified the immediate harm, a decision that required not only medical knowledge but also deep moral reflection.

The fear of being seen as a butcher also influenced these early surgeons. Many were acutely aware of the fine line they walked and struggled with the moral implications of their work. Did the potential to save a life outweigh the pain and risk they were inflicting? Could they live with the consequences if a surgery went wrong? These questions haunted many of the first surgeons, adding a layer of emotional and ethical complexity to their already challenging work.

Conclusion:

The first surgeons were pioneers in every sense of the word. They ventured into uncharted territory, armed with little more than their courage, intuition, and a few crude tools. They were revered and reviled, often in equal measure, as they navigated the treacherous path between heroism and butchery.

As we reflect on their experiences, it's important to recognise the immense challenges they faced—not just the physical challenges of performing surgery in a time before modern medicine, but also the emotional and ethical dilemmas that came with their work. These early surgeons laid the foundation for the medical advances we benefit from today, but they also remind us of the human cost of those advances.

In the end, the story of the first surgeons is one of bravery, ingenuity, and an unyielding desire to help others, even in the face of unimaginable odds. Their legacy lives on in every surgery performed today, a testament to the enduring spirit of those who dared to heal when others could not.

Chapter 4

The Evolution of Anesthesia: From Agony to Relief

Excerpt:

Imagine the terror of undergoing surgery without anesthesia—feeling every cut, every movement, every bit of pain. For centuries, this was the reality of surgery. Patients were often held down by force, their screams echoing in the operating room. But as humans, we never stopped searching for ways to ease this suffering. The discovery and evolution of anesthesia revolutionized surgery, transforming it from a nightmarish ordeal into a more humane practice.

In this chapter, we will explore:

1. **Early Pain Management:** How did ancient cultures attempt to dull pain?
2. **The Birth of Modern Anesthesia:** The key discoveries that changed everything.
3. **The Pioneers of Anesthesia:** The brave individuals who tested the unknown.
4. **The Impact on Surgery:** How anesthesia transformed the field.

The Complete Chapter:

Early Pain Management: How Did Ancient Cultures Attempt to Dull Pain?

Before the advent of modern anesthesia, pain was an inevitable part of surgery. Ancient cultures, recognizing the need to manage pain, tried various methods to dull the senses. These methods were often a mix of natural remedies, rituals, and sheer endurance.

Imagine a healer in ancient Egypt preparing a patient for surgery. They might have used a combination of opium, a powerful narcotic derived from the poppy plant, and alcohol to dull the pain. In other cultures, like those in South America, coca leaves—known for their numbing effect—were chewed or applied to wounds. The goal was simple: to ease the patient's suffering as much as possible, though these methods were far from perfect.

Other cultures turned to spiritual or psychological methods. For instance, some Native American tribes used rituals and chants to help patients enter a trance-like state, reducing their awareness of pain. In some cases, the sheer power of belief and the support of the community played a role in helping patients endure the unimaginable pain of surgery.

Despite these efforts, the reality was that surgery remained an excruciating experience for most people. The search for a more effective solution continued, driven by the deep human desire to alleviate suffering.

The Birth of Modern Anesthesia: The Key Discoveries That Changed Everything

The true revolution in anesthesia began in the 19th century, a time when science and medicine were making great strides. The key to this revolution was the discovery of substances that could reliably render a patient unconscious and insensible to pain during surgery.

One of the first breakthroughs came with the use of **ether**. In 1846, a dentist named William T.G. Morton demonstrated the use of ether as an anesthetic during a public surgery at Massachusetts General Hospital. The success of this demonstration was a turning point in the history of medicine. Ether could induce a deep, painless sleep, allowing surgeons to perform more complex procedures without causing their patients unbearable pain.

Around the same time, **chloroform** was also discovered as an effective anesthetic. It gained popularity quickly, especially in Britain, where it was famously used by Queen Victoria during the birth of her eighth child. The public endorsement of chloroform by the Queen gave it a significant boost in credibility, and it became a standard tool in the surgeon's arsenal.

These discoveries were not without their risks. Both ether and chloroform could be dangerous, sometimes leading to complications or even death. However, the benefits were undeniable. The ability to perform surgery without causing the patient extreme pain was a monumental leap forward, making it possible to save lives that might otherwise have been lost.

The Pioneers of Anesthesia: The Brave Individuals Who Tested the Unknown

The development of anesthesia wasn't just about scientific discovery—it also involved incredible bravery and determination from those who pioneered its use. These early anesthetists were often experimenting with unknown substances, uncertain of the outcomes.

One of these pioneers was **Crawford W. Long**, a country doctor in Georgia, who used ether for the first time in 1842 to remove a tumor from a patient's neck. Long didn't publish his findings until years later, meaning he missed out on some of the recognition he deserved. However, his work was vital in proving that ether could be used safely and effectively in surgery.

Another key figure was **James Young Simpson**, a Scottish obstetrician who discovered the anesthetic properties of chloroform. Simpson's willingness to experiment—sometimes even on himself—helped bring this powerful anesthetic into widespread use. His work was driven by a deep compassion for his patients, particularly women in childbirth, whom he sought to help by reducing their pain.

These pioneers faced criticism and skepticism from their peers. The idea of using substances to render patients unconscious was met with resistance by some who feared the unknown risks. But the undeniable success of anesthesia in reducing pain and improving surgical outcomes eventually won over the medical community.

The Impact on Surgery: How Anesthesia Transformed the Field

The introduction of anesthesia transformed surgery in ways that are difficult to overstate. Before anesthesia, the agony of surgery limited what surgeons could do. Operations had to be quick, as prolonged pain and shock could be fatal. This meant that many complex procedures were simply impossible.

With anesthesia, everything changed. Surgeons could take their time, performing more precise and intricate procedures. The ability to operate without causing pain opened up new possibilities for treatment, allowing for advancements in everything from orthopedic surgery to abdominal and heart surgeries.

Anesthesia also changed the patient's experience of surgery. No longer did they have to face the terror of being fully conscious during an operation. Instead, they could be put to sleep, waking up to find that the surgery was over, often with a better chance of recovery.

The psychological impact of this change was profound. Surgery, once feared and dreaded, became a more accepted and accessible option for many. This shift in perception helped pave the way for the modern era of surgery, where complex procedures are performed routinely, and the focus is on healing and recovery rather than merely surviving the ordeal.

Conclusion:

The evolution of anesthesia represents one of the most significant advancements in medical history. It took surgery from the realm of unimaginable suffering to a more humane and effective practice. The pioneers who discovered and developed anesthetics were driven by a deep desire to ease human suffering, and their work has had a lasting impact on millions of lives.

As we reflect on the history of anesthesia, it's important to remember the courage and determination of those who made it possible.

Their willingness to explore the unknown, often at great personal risk, has given us one of the most powerful tools in medicine. Thanks to their efforts, surgery has become a field where healing is not only possible but can be done with compassion and care.

Chapter 5

The Rise of Sterilization: A Battle Against the Invisible Enemy

---

Excerpt:

The world of early surgery was filled with visible challenges—pain, blood loss, and the skill of the surgeon. But lurking in the shadows was an invisible enemy that often turned successful surgeries into tragic outcomes: infection. Before the discovery of germs, many patients who survived the surgeon's knife later died from infections that no one understood. The rise of sterilization practices marked the beginning of a new era in surgery, where the focus shifted from merely surviving the operation to ensuring a full recovery.

In this chapter, we will explore:

1. **The Invisible Threat:** Understanding the problem of post-surgical infections.
2. **Ignaz Semmelweis and Hand Hygiene:** The story of a pioneer who faced resistance.
3. **Joseph Lister and Antiseptics:** How a bold idea changed the face of surgery.

4. **The Evolution of Sterilization Techniques:** From boiling instruments to modern practices.
5. **The Impact on Patient Outcomes:** How sterilization reduced mortality rates and transformed surgery.

The Complete Chapter:

The Invisible Threat: Understanding the Problem of Post-Surgical Infections

Imagine surviving a painful and dangerous surgery, only to fall ill a few days later. Your wound, instead of healing, becomes red, swollen, and foul-smelling. Fever sets in, and before long, you are fighting for your life. This was the grim reality for many patients before the rise of sterilization.

For centuries, surgeons were baffled by the infections that often followed even the most successful surgeries. They knew that something was wrong, but without an understanding of germs, they had no idea how to prevent it. Surgeons would operate in their street clothes, reuse unwashed instruments, and move from patient to patient without washing their hands. These practices were a perfect storm for spreading infections, but the connection wasn't yet understood.

Infections were the invisible enemy—silent, deadly, and largely unstoppable. For many patients, the terror of surgery didn't end when the operation was over. The threat of infection loomed large, turning the recovery period into a life-or-death struggle. The battle against this unseen foe would become one of the most important chapters in the history of surgery.

Ignaz Semmelweis and Hand Hygiene: The Story of a Pioneer Who Faced Resistance

The fight against surgical infections took a major leap forward in the mid-19th century, thanks to a Hungarian physician named Ignaz Semmelweis. Working in a Vienna hospital, Semmelweis noticed a disturbing trend: women who gave birth in the hospital's maternity ward were dying of puerperal fever at alarming rates. Yet, in another ward, where midwives delivered babies, the mortality rate was much lower.

Semmelweis made a bold connection: doctors, who often moved from performing autopsies to delivering babies without washing their hands, were carrying something from the dead bodies to the living patients. He didn't know about germs, but he theorized that some invisible substance was causing these deadly infections.

To combat this, Semmelweis introduced a simple yet revolutionary idea: handwashing. He insisted that doctors wash their hands with a chlorine solution before attending to patients. The results were dramatic—mortality rates in the maternity ward plummeted. However, despite the clear evidence, Semmelweis faced fierce resistance from his colleagues. The idea that doctors could be responsible for spreading disease was deeply offensive to many, and Semmelweis was eventually forced out of his position. It would take years for his ideas to gain the recognition they deserved.

Joseph Lister and Antiseptics: How a Bold Idea Changed the Face of Surgery

While Semmelweis laid the groundwork for the importance of hygiene, it was Joseph Lister, a British surgeon, who truly revolutionized surgical practice with the introduction of antiseptics. Inspired by Louis Pasteur's work on germ theory, Lister realized that the infections plaguing post-surgical patients were caused by microorganisms in the environment.

In the 1860s, Lister began experimenting with carbolic acid (now known as phenol) as a way to kill these germs. He applied the acid to surgical wounds, soaked instruments in it, and even sprayed it in the air of the operating room. The results were astounding—patients who had previously faced a high risk of infection began recovering without complications.

Lister's antiseptic technique marked a turning point in the history of surgery. By recognizing that invisible germs were the cause of infections and finding a way to kill them, Lister dramatically reduced post-surgical mortality rates. His work laid the foundation for modern sterilization practices and earned him a place as one of the most important figures in medical history.

The Evolution of Sterilization Techniques: From Boiling Instruments to Modern Practices

The success of Lister's antiseptic methods sparked a revolution in surgical practice. Surgeons began to understand that cleanliness was crucial not only during surgery but also in the preparation of tools and the operating environment. This led to the development of more sophisticated sterilization techniques.

In the years following Lister's discoveries, boiling instruments in water became a common practice to kill germs. This was later improved upon with the introduction of autoclaves, machines that use steam under pressure to sterilize surgical instruments and other materials. The use of sterile gloves, masks, and gowns became standard, creating a barrier between the surgeon and the patient, further reducing the risk of infection.

Modern sterilization practices have evolved to include advanced technologies like chemical sterilants, ultraviolet light, and even plasma sterilization, which uses ionized gas to kill microorganisms. These methods ensure that today's operating rooms are as free from harmful germs as possible, making surgery safer than ever before.

The Impact on Patient Outcomes: How Sterilization Reduced Mortality Rates and Transformed Surgery

The introduction and evolution of sterilization techniques had a profound impact on patient outcomes. Before sterilization, even a successful surgery could lead to a deadly infection, making recovery uncertain. But as sterilization practices became more widespread and effective, the rates of post-surgical infections plummeted.

Patients who might have once faced a high risk of death from infections like gangrene or sepsis began to recover more reliably and quickly. This not only improved individual outcomes but also increased public trust in surgical procedures. Surgery, once seen as a last resort fraught with danger, became a more accepted and routine part of medical treatment.

The rise of sterilization also allowed for more complex and invasive surgeries to be performed with greater safety. As the threat of infection diminished, surgeons could take on cases that would have been considered too risky in the past. This opened up new possibilities for medical treatment, leading to innovations that continue to save lives today.

Conclusion:

The battle against infection was one of the most critical fights in the history of surgery. The rise of sterilization transformed the field, turning surgery from a dangerous gamble into a more controlled and safer practice. The pioneering work of individuals like Ignaz Semmelweis and Joseph Lister, who saw the invisible enemy for what it was, laid the groundwork for the modern medical practices we rely on today.

Their legacy lives on in every operating room, where the principles of sterilization continue to protect patients and save lives. It's a reminder that the most powerful enemies are often those we cannot see—and that our greatest victories come from understanding and confronting them head-on. The evolution of sterilization not only changed surgery but also reshaped our approach to health and healing, making it possible to imagine a future where infection is no longer a threat to life.

Chapter 6

Surgical Innovation: The Dawn of Modern Techniques

Excerpt:

Imagine a world where the tools and techniques used in surgery were as rudimentary as they were dangerous. Early surgeons had to rely on their skill and bravery, often without the benefit of advanced instruments or techniques. But as time went on, the field of surgery began to evolve rapidly. The dawn of modern surgical techniques marked a new era, characterized by precision, safety, and a deeper understanding of human anatomy.

In this chapter, we will explore:

1. **The Birth of Modern Surgical Instruments:** How innovation transformed the tools of the trade.
2. **The Advent of Minimally Invasive Surgery:** A revolutionary approach that changed patient care.
3. **The Role of Imaging Technologies:** How advancements in imaging reshaped surgical planning and execution.

4. **The Impact of Surgical Specializations:** How focused expertise improved outcomes and broadened surgical possibilities.
5. **The Future of Surgical Innovation:** What lies ahead in the quest for better, safer surgeries?

The Complete Chapter:

The Birth of Modern Surgical Instruments: How Innovation Transformed the Tools of the Trade

Before the 19th century, surgical tools were often crude and uncomfortable. Early surgeons made do with basic knives, forceps, and saws, tools that were more suited to butchery than delicate medical procedures. These instruments, while functional, lacked the precision and safety features needed for complex surgeries.

The transformation began in the 19th century, with the development of specialized surgical instruments designed for specific procedures. Innovations like the **scalpel** with a detachable blade, the **hemostat** to control bleeding, and the **surgical needle** with a finer point significantly improved the surgeon's ability to perform precise and less traumatic operations. These advancements were driven by a growing understanding of anatomy and the need for more sophisticated tools to handle increasingly complex procedures.

In the early 20th century, the invention of **electrocautery** devices allowed surgeons to cut tissue while simultaneously cauterizing blood vessels, reducing bleeding and improving surgical outcomes. **Endoscopic instruments**, developed in the late 20th century, enabled surgeons to perform internal examinations and procedures through small incisions, marking a significant leap in surgical precision and patient recovery times.

These advancements in surgical instruments have dramatically changed the landscape of surgery. Today's tools are designed with ergonomics, precision, and safety in mind, reflecting the continued evolution of surgical practice from its more rudimentary beginnings.

The Advent of Minimally Invasive Surgery: A Revolutionary Approach That Changed Patient Care

One of the most significant leaps in modern surgery has been the advent of minimally invasive techniques. Before these techniques became widespread, surgery typically involved large incisions, leading to extended recovery times and increased risk of complications.

The concept of minimally invasive surgery (MIS) revolves around performing surgeries through small incisions, often using specialized instruments and video technology. The most notable example is **laparoscopic surgery**, which uses a thin tube with a camera (laparoscope) and small surgical instruments inserted through tiny incisions. This approach allows surgeons to view the surgical site on a monitor and perform operations with remarkable precision.

The benefits of MIS are numerous. Patients experience less pain, shorter hospital stays, and quicker recoveries compared to traditional open surgery. Additionally, the smaller incisions reduce the risk of infection and scarring, making recovery less daunting and improving overall patient satisfaction.

MIS techniques have expanded beyond the abdomen to include procedures in various areas of the body, including the heart, lungs, and even the spine. The continued innovation in this field promises to further enhance patient outcomes and redefine the possibilities of surgical treatment.

The Role of Imaging Technologies: How Advancements in Imaging Reshaped Surgical Planning and Execution

Imaging technologies have become integral to modern surgery, revolutionizing how surgeons plan and execute procedures. Before the advent of advanced imaging, surgeons relied on their understanding of anatomy and direct observation, which could sometimes lead to uncertainty during operations.

The introduction of **X-rays** in the early 20th century was a game-changer, allowing for detailed internal views of the body. Later developments like **computed tomography (CT)** and **magnetic resonance imaging (MRI)** provided even more detailed images, enabling surgeons to visualize internal structures with greater accuracy.

Ultrasound technology, which uses sound waves to create images of internal organs, has become a vital tool in both diagnosis and intraoperative guidance. Surgeons can use real-time ultrasound to navigate complex procedures and ensure accuracy.

These imaging technologies have greatly enhanced surgical precision, allowing for better preoperative planning, more accurate targeting of surgical sites, and improved postoperative assessments. By integrating these technologies into surgical practice, surgeons can reduce risks, optimize outcomes, and provide patients with a higher standard of care.

The Impact of Surgical Specializations: How Focused Expertise Improved Outcomes and Broadened Surgical Possibilities

As surgery evolved, so did the need for specialized knowledge and skills. The development of surgical specializations allowed for a more focused approach to complex procedures, leading to better outcomes and more innovative techniques.

Surgeons began to focus on specific areas of the body or types of procedures, leading to the rise of fields such as **neurosurgery**, **cardiothoracic surgery**, and **orthopedic surgery**. Each specialization required extensive training and expertise, leading to advancements in techniques and technologies tailored to particular types of surgery.

The specialization of surgery has allowed for a deeper understanding of complex conditions and more effective treatment options. Surgeons specializing in specific areas can provide more precise and targeted care, often leading to improved patient outcomes and reduced complication rates.

Specialized surgical centers and teams have become common, bringing together experts in various fields to address complex cases. This collaborative approach ensures that patients receive comprehensive care tailored to their specific needs, reflecting the ongoing advancement and refinement of surgical practice.

The Future of Surgical Innovation: What Lies Ahead in the Quest for Better, Safer Surgeries?

The field of surgery continues to evolve, with ongoing research and innovation promising exciting developments. One area of significant potential is **robot-assisted surgery**, which uses robotic systems to enhance precision and control during procedures. These systems offer surgeons greater dexterity and accuracy, potentially improving outcomes and reducing recovery times.

Another promising area is **regenerative medicine**, which focuses on repairing or replacing damaged tissues and organs using techniques like stem cell therapy. This approach has the potential to revolutionize the treatment of injuries and diseases, providing new options for patients who previously had limited choices.

Artificial intelligence (AI) and **machine learning** are also making their mark on surgery, with algorithms being developed to assist in diagnosis, surgical planning, and even real-time decision-making during procedures. These technologies promise to further enhance surgical precision and personalize patient care.

As we look to the future, the quest for better, safer surgeries continues. The integration of advanced technologies, ongoing research, and the commitment of the surgical community to innovation will drive the next generation of surgical practices, improving outcomes and expanding the possibilities of what can be achieved.

Conclusion:

The dawn of modern surgical techniques represents a remarkable journey from the rudimentary tools and practices of early surgery to the advanced, precise methods we use today. Innovations in surgical instruments, minimally invasive techniques, imaging technologies, and specialized expertise have transformed the field, making surgery safer, more effective, and more patient-centered.

As we continue to push the boundaries of what is possible, the future of surgery holds exciting possibilities. The ongoing drive for innovation and improvement reflects the commitment of the surgical community to advancing patient care and achieving better outcomes. The journey from the past to the present is a testament to human ingenuity and the relentless pursuit of progress in the quest to heal and save lives.

Chapter 7

The Role of Technology in Revolutionizing Surgery

Excerpt:

Imagine stepping into a futuristic operating room where technology seamlessly integrates with human skill to perform complex procedures with unprecedented precision. From robotic assistants to advanced imaging systems, technology has transformed surgery into a field characterized by innovation and accuracy. As we delve into this chapter, we'll explore how technological advancements have reshaped surgical practice, making procedures safer, more efficient, and tailored to individual patient needs.

In this chapter, we will explore:

1. **The Emergence of Robotic Surgery:** How robots are changing the landscape of surgical procedures.
2. **Advancements in Imaging Technologies:** The role of cutting-edge imaging in enhancing surgical precision.
3. **The Impact of Simulation and Training Technologies:** How virtual reality and simulations are improving surgical skills.

4. **The Integration of Artificial Intelligence:** The potential of AI to enhance decision-making and surgical outcomes.
5. **The Future of Surgical Technology:** What lies ahead in the realm of surgical innovation?

The Complete Chapter:

The Emergence of Robotic Surgery: How Robots Are Changing the Landscape of Surgical Procedures

Imagine a world where surgery isn't just about the skill of the surgeon, but also about the precision of robotic technology. Robotic surgery, or **robot-assisted surgery**, represents one of the most significant advancements in modern medicine. These systems combine the expertise of human surgeons with the precision of robotic instruments to enhance surgical outcomes.

One of the most well-known robotic systems is the **da Vinci Surgical System**, which allows surgeons to perform minimally invasive procedures with unparalleled accuracy. The robot's arms are equipped with tiny, precise instruments and a high-definition camera, enabling the surgeon to control them through a console. This setup allows for smaller incisions and more intricate manoeuvres than traditional methods.

The benefits of robotic surgery are substantial. It offers greater dexterity and range of motion compared to human hands alone, allowing for complex procedures to be performed with precision. Additionally, patients often experience shorter recovery times, less pain, and reduced risk of complications due to the minimally invasive nature of the procedures.

However, robotic surgery also comes with challenges. The technology is expensive, and there is a learning curve for surgeons who must master both the robotic system and its integration with their surgical techniques. Despite these challenges, the continued development of robotic surgery promises to push the boundaries of what is possible in the operating room.

Advancements in Imaging Technologies: The Role of Cutting-Edge Imaging in Enhancing Surgical Precision

Imaging technologies have revolutionized the way surgeons plan and execute procedures. Before advanced imaging, surgeons had to rely on their knowledge of anatomy and direct observation, which could sometimes lead to less-than-ideal outcomes. Today, technologies such as **computed tomography (CT)**, **magnetic resonance imaging (MRI)**, and **ultrasound** provide detailed and precise images of the body's internal structures.

CT scans offer cross-sectional views of the body, allowing surgeons to see inside the patient with remarkable clarity. This technology is particularly useful for planning complex surgeries, as it helps visualize the exact location and extent of tumors, fractures, or other conditions.

MRI provides detailed images of soft tissues, such as the brain, spinal cord, and muscles, offering insights that are crucial for surgeries involving these areas. MRI's ability to differentiate between different types of tissue makes it invaluable for planning and executing intricate procedures.

Ultrasound imaging uses sound waves to create real-time images of internal organs. This technology is especially useful during minimally invasive procedures, as it allows surgeons to guide instruments accurately and make adjustments based on live feedback.

These imaging technologies have significantly improved surgical precision. By providing detailed views of the surgical site, they enable more accurate planning and execution, leading to better outcomes and reduced risk of complications.

The Impact of Simulation and Training Technologies: How Virtual Reality and Simulations Are Improving Surgical Skills

In the world of surgery, practice makes perfect, and technology has provided new ways to practice and refine surgical skills. **Simulation and training**

technologies have become essential tools for preparing surgeons for real-life procedures.

Virtual reality (VR) and **augmented reality (AR)** offer immersive training environments where surgeons can practice complex procedures without the risk of harming patients. VR simulations create realistic surgical scenarios where trainees can perform operations in a controlled setting. This hands-on experience helps build confidence and skill before entering the operating room.

Surgical simulators are another valuable tool. These devices mimic the feel and resistance of real tissues, allowing surgeons to practice techniques and develop their skills. They provide immediate feedback, helping trainees identify and correct mistakes in a safe and controlled environment.

These technologies have transformed surgical training by providing realistic and effective ways to practice and perfect skills. Surgeons can now gain experience and confidence before performing procedures on actual patients, leading to improved performance and patient outcomes.

The Integration of Artificial Intelligence: The Potential of AI to Enhance Decision-Making and Surgical Outcomes

Artificial intelligence (AI) is making waves across various fields, and surgery is no exception. AI's ability to analyze vast amounts of data quickly and accurately offers exciting possibilities for enhancing surgical practice.

One application of AI in surgery is **decision support systems**, which analyze patient data to provide recommendations for surgical planning and execution. These systems can suggest optimal surgical approaches, predict potential complications, and even assist in real-time decision-making during procedures.

AI algorithms can also be used for **image analysis**, helping to identify anomalies or patterns that might be missed by the human eye. This capability is particularly useful in diagnosing conditions and guiding surgical interventions.

Additionally, AI-driven **robotic systems** are enhancing surgical precision and control. These systems can assist in complex procedures by providing real-time feedback and adjusting techniques based on data analysis.

The integration of AI into surgery promises to improve outcomes and safety by augmenting the surgeon's expertise with data-driven insights and advanced technology. As AI continues to evolve, its role in surgery will likely expand, leading to even greater advancements in the field.

The Future of Surgical Technology: What Lies Ahead in the Realm of Surgical Innovation?

The future of surgical technology is bright, with numerous innovations on the horizon. **Robotic systems** are expected to become more advanced, offering even greater precision and capabilities. Future robots may incorporate AI and machine learning to further enhance their functionality.

Regenerative medicine and **tissue engineering** are also promising areas of development. These fields focus on repairing or replacing damaged tissues and organs, potentially transforming the way we approach surgical treatment.

Wearable technology and **remote surgery** are other exciting prospects. Wearables could monitor patients' health in real-time, providing valuable data for surgical planning and recovery. Remote surgery, enabled by advanced communication and robotic technology, could allow surgeons to perform procedures from a distance, offering new possibilities for global healthcare access.

As we look to the future, the continued evolution of surgical technology promises to push the boundaries of what is possible, improving patient care and outcomes. The ongoing drive for innovation reflects the dedication of the surgical community to advancing the field and achieving new levels of precision and effectiveness.

Conclusion:

The role of technology in revolutionizing surgery represents a remarkable journey from basic tools and techniques to advanced, precise, and patient-centred practices. Robotic systems, imaging technologies, simulation and training tools, and artificial intelligence have all played a crucial role in transforming surgical practice.

As we continue to embrace and integrate new technologies, the future of surgery holds exciting possibilities. The relentless pursuit of innovation reflects a commitment to improving patient care and achieving better outcomes. The story of surgical technology is one of progress, ingenuity, and a deep dedication to enhancing the art and science of healing.

Chapter 8

The Ethics of Surgery: Balancing Innovation with Responsibility

---

Excerpt:

Surgery is a field marked by incredible advancements and breakthroughs, but it also raises profound ethical questions. As we push the boundaries of what is possible, we must navigate complex issues related to patient care, consent, and the responsible use of technology. This chapter delves into the ethical considerations that accompany surgical practice, exploring how innovation intersects with the principles of medical ethics.

In this chapter, we will explore:

1. **Informed Consent and Patient Autonomy:** The importance of ensuring patients understand and agree to their treatment.
2. **Balancing Risk and Benefit:** How surgeons weigh the potential outcomes of a procedure.
3. **The Role of Technology in Ethical Decision-Making:** Navigating the ethical implications of advanced technologies.

4. **Access and Equity in Surgical Care:** Addressing disparities in access to surgical treatments.
5. **The Future of Surgical Ethics:** Emerging ethical challenges as the field continues to evolve.

The Complete Chapter:

Informed Consent and Patient Autonomy: The Importance of Ensuring Patients Understand and Agree to Their Treatment

Informed consent is a cornerstone of medical ethics, and it's especially crucial in surgery, where procedures can be complex and risky. Informed consent ensures that patients are fully aware of what a surgery entails and agree to proceed based on a clear understanding of the potential risks and benefits.

For patients, this means having a detailed discussion with their surgeon about the procedure, including what it involves, possible complications, and expected outcomes. Surgeons must present this information in a way that is understandable and free of medical jargon. It's not just about giving patients a list of risks and benefits; it's about ensuring they have the opportunity to ask questions and express concerns.

Patient autonomy is the principle that individuals have the right to make their own decisions about their healthcare. This means respecting a patient's choices, even if they choose to decline a recommended surgery. It's important for patients to feel empowered and informed, allowing them to make decisions that align with their values and preferences.

Ethical dilemmas can arise if patients are not fully informed or if there's pressure to proceed with a surgery that might not align with their personal values. Ensuring informed consent is not just a legal requirement; it's a fundamental aspect of respecting patients' rights and promoting ethical medical practice.

Balancing Risk and Benefit: How Surgeons Weigh the Potential Outcomes of a Procedure

Surgery inherently involves risks, and surgeons must carefully weigh these risks against the potential benefits. This process involves assessing the likelihood of success, possible complications, and the impact on the patient's quality of life.

Surgeons must consider various factors, including the patient's overall health, the severity of their condition, and the potential for recovery. They use their expertise and experience to evaluate whether the benefits of the surgery outweigh the risks. This requires not only technical skill but also a deep understanding of the patient's unique situation and preferences.

In some cases, surgeons might face difficult decisions, such as whether to recommend a high-risk surgery for a patient with a serious condition.

These decisions require careful consideration and honest discussions with patients about the potential outcomes. Balancing risk and benefit is a crucial aspect of ethical decision-making in surgery.

Surgeons also need to be transparent about the potential risks and uncertainties. Providing a realistic assessment of the chances of success and possible complications helps patients make informed choices about their treatment options.

The Role of Technology in Ethical Decision-Making: Navigating the Ethical Implications of Advanced Technologies

As surgical technology advances, new ethical questions arise. Technologies like robotic surgery, AI-driven decision support, and advanced imaging systems offer incredible potential but also come with ethical considerations.

For instance, robotic surgery can enhance precision and reduce recovery times, but it also raises questions about the implications of replacing human skill with machines. There's a need to ensure that these technologies are used responsibly and that they complement rather than replace the critical judgment and expertise of human surgeons.

AI in surgery presents its own set of ethical challenges. While AI can analyze vast amounts of data and offer valuable insights, it's crucial to ensure that AI systems are used ethically and that their recommendations are interpreted and validated by experienced surgeons. There's also the issue of data privacy and ensuring that patient information is handled securely.

Technological advancements can sometimes lead to a focus on innovation at the expense of patient care. It's essential to maintain a balance between leveraging new technologies and adhering to the core principles of medical ethics, such as patient well-being, safety, and respect for individual autonomy.

Access and Equity in Surgical Care: Addressing Disparities in Access to Surgical Treatments

Access to surgical care is not always equal, and disparities can exist based on factors like socioeconomic status, geographic location, and healthcare infrastructure. Addressing these disparities is a key ethical issue in modern surgery.

In many parts of the world, access to advanced surgical procedures and technologies is limited, leading to inequalities in the quality of care. Efforts to improve access to surgical care include increasing funding for healthcare infrastructure, providing training for healthcare professionals in underserved areas, and developing policies to ensure that surgical care is accessible to all individuals, regardless of their background.

Ethical considerations also involve addressing the needs of marginalized populations and ensuring that everyone has the opportunity to benefit from advancements in surgical technology. This requires a commitment to equity and justice in healthcare, working to bridge gaps and provide high-quality care to all patients.

The Future of Surgical Ethics: Emerging Ethical Challenges as the Field Continues to Evolve

As surgery continues to evolve, new ethical challenges are likely to emerge. Innovations in fields like regenerative medicine, personalized surgery, and remote surgery will bring new questions about the ethical implications of these advancements.

For example, regenerative medicine holds promise for treating previously untreatable conditions, but it also raises ethical questions about the use of stem cells and genetic modifications. Personalized surgery, which tailors procedures to individual patients based on genetic and other data, will require careful consideration of privacy and consent.

Remote surgery, enabled by advancements in communication and robotics, presents opportunities for expanding access to care but also raises concerns about the quality of care and the potential for miscommunication between surgeons and patients.

The future of surgical ethics will involve navigating these and other emerging issues, ensuring that technological advancements are used responsibly and that patient welfare remains at the forefront of surgical practice. It will require ongoing dialogue, reflection, and adaptation to maintain the balance between innovation and ethical responsibility.

Conclusion:

The ethics of surgery is a complex and evolving field, shaped by the need to balance innovation with responsibility. Informed consent, risk and benefit assessment, the role of technology, access and equity, and emerging ethical challenges are all critical aspects of modern surgical practice.

As we continue to advance the field of surgery, maintaining a focus on ethical principles is essential to ensure that patient care remains compassionate, respectful, and equitable. The journey of surgical ethics reflects our commitment to upholding the values of integrity and responsibility as we push the boundaries of what is possible in medicine.

Chapter 9

The Global Impact of Surgical Advancements: Bridging Borders in Medical Innovation

---

Excerpt:

Surgical advancements have transformed the way we approach medicine, but their impact reaches far beyond individual operating rooms. From enhancing global health to shaping international collaboration, these innovations are bridging gaps and extending their benefits across borders. This chapter delves into how surgical progress is influencing healthcare on a global scale and explores the interconnected world of medical innovation.

In this chapter, we will explore:

1. **Global Health Initiatives and Surgical Innovation:** How advancements are contributing to global health efforts.
2. **International Collaboration in Surgical Research:** The role of cross-border partnerships in driving innovation.
3. **The Spread of Surgical Technologies:** How new techniques and tools are being adopted worldwide.

4. **Challenges and Opportunities in Global Surgery:** Addressing disparities and leveraging advancements for global benefit.
5. **The Future of Global Surgical Impact:** Envisioning a world where surgical innovations are accessible to all.

The Complete Chapter:

Global Health Initiatives and Surgical Innovation: How Advancements Are Contributing to Global Health Efforts

Surgical advancements play a crucial role in global health initiatives, addressing some of the most pressing health challenges faced by populations around the world. Organizations like the **World Health Organization (WHO)** and various non-governmental organizations (NGOs) work to improve surgical care in low-resource settings, aiming to enhance outcomes and save lives.

Innovations such as **basic surgical kits**, designed for use in resource-limited environments, have made a significant impact. These kits contain essential tools and are often part of initiatives aimed at improving surgical care in underserved areas. They enable healthcare providers to perform life-saving procedures in conditions where traditional resources might be scarce.

Another significant advancement is the development of **field hospitals** and **mobile surgical units**, which bring surgical care to remote and conflict-affected regions. These units are equipped with the latest technologies and staffed by teams of skilled surgeons who can provide emergency care and routine surgeries in areas with limited access to healthcare facilities.

Global health initiatives also focus on training and capacity-building. By providing education and resources to healthcare workers in developing countries, these programs help improve surgical techniques and expand access to care. This approach not only addresses immediate health needs but also builds long-term healthcare infrastructure.

International Collaboration in Surgical Research: The Role of Cross-Border Partnerships in Driving Innovation

International collaboration is a key driver of progress in surgical research and innovation. Researchers and clinicians from different countries come together to share knowledge, resources, and expertise, leading to groundbreaking advancements and improvements in surgical practice.

Global conferences and **research networks** facilitate these collaborations, allowing professionals from around the world to exchange ideas and work on joint projects. These partnerships enable the sharing of best practices, research findings, and technological advancements, accelerating the pace of innovation.

For instance, **clinical trials** often involve multiple countries, providing diverse data and perspectives that enhance the reliability and applicability of findings. By working together, researchers can address complex challenges and develop solutions that benefit patients globally.

International collaborations also foster the development of **global guidelines and standards**, ensuring that advancements in surgical care are implemented consistently and effectively across different regions. These efforts contribute to the overall improvement of surgical practice and patient outcomes worldwide.

The Spread of Surgical Technologies: How New Techniques and Tools Are Being Adopted Worldwide

The adoption of new surgical technologies has expanded significantly, with innovations spreading across borders and becoming more accessible to healthcare providers worldwide. Technologies that were once limited to well-funded hospitals are now reaching facilities in developing countries, thanks to efforts to improve accessibility and affordability.

Telemedicine and **tele-surgery** are prime examples of how technology is bridging gaps in access to care. These systems allow specialists to consult on cases remotely, providing guidance and support to surgeons in distant locations. This capability enhances the quality of care and expands access to expert advice, even in areas with limited surgical resources.

Robotic surgery and **minimally invasive techniques** are also being adopted globally, though the rate of adoption varies. Efforts are being made to make these technologies more affordable and accessible to healthcare systems around the world. Initiatives such as **training programs** and **partnerships with local institutions** help spread these innovations and ensure that they are utilized effectively.

The global spread of surgical technologies reflects a growing recognition of the need to address health disparities and provide high-quality care regardless of geographical location. As technologies become more widely available, they hold the potential to significantly improve surgical outcomes and patient care across the globe.

Challenges and Opportunities in Global Surgery: Addressing Disparities and Leveraging Advancements for Global Benefit

While the advancements in surgical technology offer tremendous potential, they also present challenges, particularly in addressing disparities in access to care. In many parts of the world, disparities in healthcare infrastructure, training, and resources can limit the benefits of these innovations.

One major challenge is ensuring that surgical advancements reach underserved populations. Efforts are needed to address issues such as **infrastructure limitations**, **lack of trained personnel**, and **financial constraints** that can hinder the delivery of high-quality surgical care.

Opportunities exist to overcome these challenges through **global partnerships**, **capacity-building initiatives**, and **innovative solutions**. For example, organizations are working to develop affordable surgical technologies, provide training to healthcare workers, and improve healthcare infrastructure in low-resource settings.

By addressing these disparities and leveraging advancements, the global surgical community can work towards achieving more equitable access to care and improving health outcomes worldwide. Collaborative efforts and a commitment to addressing these challenges are essential for maximizing the impact of surgical innovations.

The Future of Global Surgical Impact: Envisioning a World Where Surgical Innovations Are Accessible to All

Looking to the future, the goal is to create a world where surgical innovations are accessible to all individuals, regardless of their location or socioeconomic status. This vision involves continued efforts to expand access to advanced technologies, improve healthcare infrastructure, and address health disparities.

Global initiatives and **collaborative research** will play a crucial role in achieving this vision. By fostering international partnerships and investing in healthcare systems, we can work towards making high-quality surgical care a reality for everyone.

Emerging technologies such as **3D printing**, **regenerative medicine**, and **AI-driven tools** hold promise for further advancing surgical practice and expanding access. The continued development and implementation of these technologies will shape the future of global surgery and drive improvements in patient care.

As we move forward, the focus must remain on ensuring that surgical advancements benefit all individuals and contribute to a healthier, more equitable world. The commitment to global health and collaboration will be key in realizing this vision and achieving a future where surgical innovations are accessible and impactful for everyone.

Conclusion:

The global impact of surgical advancements is a testament to the power of innovation and collaboration in improving healthcare worldwide. From global health initiatives to international research partnerships, these advancements are bridging borders and extending their benefits across the globe.

By addressing challenges and leveraging opportunities, the global surgical community can work towards a future where high-quality surgical care is accessible to all. The journey of surgical innovation is one of progress, interconnectedness, and a shared commitment to enhancing health and well-being on a global scale.

Epilogue

Reflections on the Journey of Surgical Innovation

Excerpt:

As we reach the end of our exploration into the invention of surgery, we stand at a fascinating juncture where the past, present, and future of this field intersect. The journey of surgical innovation is not merely a story of technological advancement but also one of human perseverance, creativity, and compassion. This epilogue reflects on the profound impact of surgery on our lives and envisions the continued evolution of this remarkable field.

In this epilogue, we will reflect on:

1. **The Human Element in Surgical Progress:** How the dedication and ingenuity of individuals have shaped the field.
2. **The Impact of Surgical Innovation on Modern Medicine:** The transformative effects of advancements on patient care and outcomes.
3. **The Ethical and Global Considerations:** How ethical considerations and global collaboration continue to influence surgical practice.

4. **Looking Ahead: The Future of Surgery:** Envisioning the potential future developments and their implications for healthcare.
5. **A Tribute to the Unsung Heroes:** Recognizing the contributions of those who work behind the scenes to make surgical advancements possible.

The Complete Epilogue:

The Human Element in Surgical Progress: How the Dedication and Ingenuity of Individuals Have Shaped the Field

The journey of surgical innovation is deeply intertwined with the stories of remarkable individuals whose dedication and ingenuity have propelled the field forward. From ancient pioneers who used rudimentary tools to modern surgeons pushing the boundaries of technology, the human element has been a driving force in the evolution of surgery.

Surgeons, researchers, and inventors have faced countless challenges and setbacks, yet their perseverance and creativity have led to groundbreaking advancements. Figures like **Hippocrates**, **Joseph Lister**, and **Paul Ehrlich** made significant contributions that transformed the practice of surgery. Their commitment to improving patient care and advancing medical knowledge is a testament to the enduring spirit of innovation.

Every surgical breakthrough is built upon the efforts of countless individuals who have dedicated their lives to understanding the complexities of the human body and developing new techniques. The field of surgery is a collective achievement, reflecting the passion and ingenuity of those who have come before us and continue to shape its future.

The Impact of Surgical Innovation on Modern Medicine: The Transformative Effects of Advancements on Patient Care and Outcomes

Surgical innovation has had a profound impact on modern medicine, revolutionizing the way we approach patient care and treatment. The development of **minimally invasive techniques**, **robotic surgery**, and **advanced imaging technologies** has transformed the field, offering new possibilities for improving patient outcomes.

These advancements have led to shorter recovery times, reduced complications, and enhanced precision in surgical procedures. Patients now benefit from treatments that were once considered impossible, and the quality of care has reached new heights.

For example, **laparoscopic surgery** allows for smaller incisions and quicker recovery, while **robotic-assisted surgeries** provide unparalleled precision and control. The integration of **imaging technologies** such as MRI and CT scans has enabled surgeons to visualize and plan procedures with remarkable accuracy.

The impact of these innovations extends beyond the operating room, influencing the overall trajectory of patient care and recovery. Surgical advancements have not only improved individual outcomes but have also contributed to the broader goals of modern medicine, such as reducing hospital stays and enhancing quality of life.

The Ethical and Global Considerations: How Ethical Considerations and Global Collaboration Continue to Influence Surgical Practice

As surgical techniques and technologies continue to advance, ethical considerations and global collaboration play a crucial role in shaping the field. The ethical dimensions of surgery involve ensuring that innovations are used responsibly, with a focus on patient welfare and equity.

Informed consent, **risk assessment**, and **access to care** are key ethical concerns that must be addressed as the field evolves. Surgeons and researchers must navigate these issues with sensitivity and integrity, ensuring that advancements benefit patients while respecting their rights and autonomy.

Global collaboration is essential for addressing disparities in surgical care and advancing the field on a worldwide scale. Efforts to improve access to surgical technologies and training in underserved regions are vital for promoting equity and enhancing global health.

International partnerships and cross-border research contribute to a collective effort to address health challenges and share knowledge. By working together, the global surgical community can leverage innovations to benefit patients around the world and advance the field in a responsible and ethical manner.

Looking Ahead: The Future of Surgery: Envisioning the Potential Future Developments and Their Implications for Healthcare

The future of surgery holds exciting possibilities as new discoveries and technologies continue to emerge. **Genetic engineering**, **regenerative medicine**, and **nanotechnology** are poised to revolutionize the field, offering new approaches to treatment and repair.

Genetic engineering may enable personalized treatments tailored to individual genetic profiles, while **regenerative medicine** has the potential to repair or replace damaged tissues and organs. **Nanotechnology** could lead to innovations in minimally invasive procedures and targeted drug delivery.

These advancements promise to further enhance surgical capabilities and improve patient outcomes. The integration of new technologies will likely bring about significant changes in how surgeries are performed and how patients are treated, offering hope for even greater progress in the future.

As we look ahead, the focus will be on harnessing these advancements to continue improving patient care, addressing health disparities, and expanding access to cutting-edge treatments. The future of surgery is bright, with the potential to transform the field and contribute to a healthier, more equitable world.

A Tribute to the Unsung Heroes: Recognizing the Contributions of Those Who Work Behind the Scenes to Make Surgical Advancements Possible

The progress of surgical innovation is made possible by the efforts of many individuals who work behind the scenes. From **medical researchers** and **engineers** to **nurses** and **support staff**, these unsung heroes play a crucial role in advancing the field.

Their contributions often go unnoticed, but they are essential to the success of surgical advancements. Researchers develop new technologies and techniques, engineers design and build sophisticated tools, and nurses and support staff provide vital care and support to patients undergoing surgery.

In recognizing their contributions, we acknowledge the collaborative effort that drives the field of surgery forward. Their dedication and hard work are integral to the continued progress and success of surgical practice.

Conclusion:

The journey of surgical innovation is a remarkable story of human ingenuity, dedication, and compassion. From its early beginnings to the cutting-edge advancements of today, surgery has continually evolved, transforming patient care and medical practice.

As we reflect on this journey, we celebrate the progress made and look forward to the future with optimism and excitement. The field of surgery will continue to advance, driven by the collective efforts of individuals committed to improving health and well-being.

The story of surgery is one of progress, collaboration, and hope. It is a testament to the power of human ingenuity and the enduring quest to heal and enhance lives.

9 789394 234116

Printed at Repro India Ltd.